ALETOPELTA

and Other Dinosaurs of the West Coast

by Dougal Dixon

illustrated by
Steve Weston and James Field

PICTURE WINDOW BOOKS
Minneapolis, Minnesota

Picture Window Books
5115 Excelsior Boulevard
Suite 232
Minneapolis, MN 55416
877-845-8392
www.picturewindowbooks.com

Printed in the United States of America.

Library of Congress Cataloging-in-Publication Data
Dixon, Dougal.
Aletopelta and other dinosaurs of the West coast /
by Dougal Dixon ; illustrated by Steve Weston &
James Field.
p. cm. — (Dinosaur find)
Includes bibliographical references and index.
ISBN-13: 978-1-4048-2744-8 (hardcover)
ISBN-10: 1-4048-2744-7 (hardcover)
1. Aletopelta—Juvenile literature. 2. Dinosaurs—West
(U.S.)—Juvenile literature. 3. Dinosaurs—California,
Southern—Juvenile literature. I. Weston, Steve, ill. II.
Field, James, 1959– ill. III. Title. IV. Series: Dixon, Dougal.
Dinosaur find.
QE862.O65D585 2007
567.90979—dc22   2006012130

Acknowledgments
This book was produced for Picture Window Books by
Bender Richardson White, U.K.

Illustrations by James Field (cover and pages 4–5, 9,
15, 17, 21) and Steve Weston (pages 7, 11, 13, 19).
Diagrams by Stefan Chabluk.

Photographs: Eyewire Inc. pages 8, 10, 12, 14, 16, 18;
iStockphoto pages 6 (Jordan Cutler), 20 (Vera
Bogaerts).

Consultant: John Stidworthy, Scientific Fellow of
the Zoological Society, London, and former
Lecturer in the Education Department, Natural
History Museum, London.

Reading Adviser: Susan Kesselring, M.A., Literacy
Educator, Rosemount–Apple Valley–Eagan
(Minnesota) School District

Types of dinosaurs
In this book, a red shape at the top of a left-hand page shows the animal was a meat-eater. A green shape shows it was a plant-eater.

Just how big—or small— were they?
Dinosaurs were many different sizes. We have compared their sizes to one of the following:

 Chicken
2 feet (60 centimeters) tall
6 pounds (2.7 kilograms)

Adult person
6 feet (1.8 meters) tall
170 pounds (76.5 kg)

 Elephant
10 feet (3 m) tall
12,000 pounds
(5,400 kg)

TABLE OF CONTENTS

WHAT'S INSIDE?

Dinosaurs! These dinosaurs lived on what is now the West Coast of North America. Find out how they survived millions of years ago and what they have in common with today's animals.

LIFE ON THE WEST COAST

Dinosaurs lived between 230 million and 65 million years ago. The world did not look the same then. Much of the land and many of the seas were not in the same places as today. However, the West Coast of North America was a little like today, with the Pacific Ocean to the west and mountains just inland.

Along the ancient West Coast, meat-eating dinosaurs like *Albertosaurus* and *Labocania* hunted the plant-eaters. Among the plant-eating dinosaurs were duck-billed *Lambeosaurus* and armored *Aletopelta*.

SAUROLOPHUS

Pronunciation:
SAW-ro-LO-fus

Saurolophus was one of the duck-billed dinosaurs. It had a broad, duck-like beak, or bill, as its mouth and jaws. *Saurolophus* used its bill to tear up big mouthfuls of plants. It could hold the food in its cheeks while it chewed.

Big mouth today

The moose has a broad mouth and wide cheeks, just like *Saurolophus* had. The cheeks hold the food while the moose chews it.

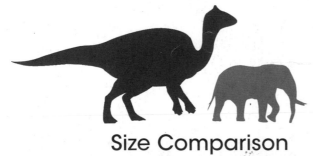

Size Comparison

Saurolophus lived in groups in the woodlands, coming out into the open to drink.

LAMBEOSAURUS

Pronunciation:
LAM-bee-o-SAW-rus

The crest of *Lambeosaurus* was a different shape and size than the crests of other duck-billed dinosaurs. The crest was a growth on its head. It had a hollow square part and a solid spike at the back. Duck-billed dinosaurs could tell each other apart by their crests.

Ornamented heads today

Hoofed animals like the elk have different shaped antlers. The antlers help them recognize their own kind, just like the crest of *Lambeosaurus* did.

Size Comparison

Lambeosaurus fed on the leaves of woodland trees. It may have made sounds with its crest to signal to other dinosaurs.

HYPSILOPHODON

Pronunciation:
HIP-sih-LO-fo-dahn

Hypsilophodon was one of the smaller plant-eating dinosaurs. It nibbled leaves and twigs from bushes and from the plants that grew in the undergrowth. Its dark colors and stripes helped it hide from hungry meat-eaters.

Small plant-eaters today

The wild turkey is dark colored and eats plants that grow close to the ground, just like *Hypsilophodon* did.

Size Comparison

10

Hypsilophodon usually blended into its surroundings. But if spotted by a meat-eating dinosaur, it used its long legs to run away.

PANOPLOSAURUS

Pronunciation:
PAN-o-plo-SAW-rus

Panoplosaurus was one of the armored dinosaurs. Its back was covered with a jigsaw of shields and plates that protected it from attack. Unlike other armored dinosaurs, *Panoplosaurus* had no horns or spikes to use as weapons.

Armor today

The armor of *Panoplosaurus* looked much like that of today's armadillo.

Size Comparison

Panoplosaurus lived in the woodlands but would go out into the open to look for different foods.

LABOCANIA

Pronunciation:
LAB-o-KAN-ee-uh

Labocania was a huge, fierce predator. It hunted the duck-billed dinosaurs and other plant-eaters that lived on the West Coast. It had big jaws and sharp teeth like a *Tyrannosaurus*.

Fierce hunter today

The timber wolf prowls through mountain woodlands and forests, hunting big animals, like *Labocania* did.

Size Comparison

Labocania used its good eyesight to find its prey. It could sneak up on big animals through the trees.

ALETOPELTA

Mountain-dwelling *Aletopelta* was covered in armor. It had heavy shields and spikes around its neck and shoulders. The rest of its back was covered with small armor lumps. Plates stuck up along the dinosaur's tail.

Mountain-dweller today

The Rocky Mountain goat lives on mountainsides, like *Aletopelta* did.

Size Comparison

Aletopelta fed on ferns in the mountain meadows. It used its armor for defense against meat-eaters, not for attack.

17

SAURORNITHOLESTES

Pronunciation:
SAWR-or-NITH-o-LES-tees

Saurornitholestes was one of the smaller meat-eating dinosaurs of the West Coast. It hunted animals such as lizards and small mammals. It chased them on its long hind legs and killed them with the big claws on its feet.

Clawed hunter today

The bald eagle sometimes uses its claws to kill prey. It is about the same size as *Saurornitholestes* was.

Size Comparison

Saurornitholestes hunted for animals in the rocky ravines and gullies at the foot of the mountains.

ALBERTOSAURUS

Pronunciation:
al-BUR-tuh-SAW-rus

Albertosaurus was the biggest meat-eater of the West Coast at the end of the Age of Dinosaurs. It hunted all of the other animals, big or small. It even may have eaten animals that were already dead.

Scavenging today

The grizzly bear is the biggest hunter of the West Coast today. Like *Albertosaurus*, it also scavenges for food.

Size Comparison

Albertosaurus may have scavenged the dead animals that washed up on the beaches.

21

WHERE DID THEY GO?

Dinosaurs are extinct, which means that none of them are alive today. Scientists study rocks and fossils to find clues about what happened to dinosaurs.

People have different explanations about what happened. Some people think a huge asteroid hit Earth and caused all sorts of climate changes, which caused the dinosaurs to die. Others think volcanic eruptions caused the climate to change and that killed the dinosaurs. No one knows for sure what happened to all of the dinosaurs.

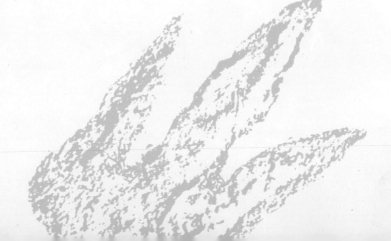

GLOSSARY

armor—protective covering of plates, horns, spikes, or clubs used for fighting

bill—the hard front part of the mouth of birds and some dinosaurs; also called a beak

crest—a structure on top of the head, usually used to signal to other animals

ferns—plants with finely divided leaves known as fronds; ferns are common in damp woods and along rivers

inland—away from the shore

mammals—warm-blooded animals that have hair and drink mother's milk when they are young

prey—animals that are hunted by other animals for food; the hunters are known as predators

scavenges—feeds on animals that are already dead

signal—to make a sign, warning, or hint

To Learn More

At the Library

Clark, Neil, and William Lindsay. *1001 Facts About Dinosaurs.* New York: Backpack Books, Dorling Kindersley, 2002.

Lessem, Don. *Armored Dinosaurs.* Minneapolis: Lerner Publications, 2005.

Levin, Freddie. *1-2-3 Draw Dinosaurs and Other Prehistoric Animals.* Columbus, N.C.: Peel Productions, 2000.

On the Web

FactHound offers a safe, fun way to find Internet sites related to this book. All of the sites on FactHound have been researched by our staff.

1. Visit *www.facthound.com*

2. Type in this special code for age-appropriate sites: 1404827447

3. Click on the FETCH IT button.

Your trusty FactHound will fetch the best sites for you!

Index

Look for all of the books in the Dinosaur Find series: